Slave Narratives: A Folk History of Slavery in the United States, From Interviews with Former Slaves:
Virginia Interviews
By
Works Progress Administration

VIRGINIA SLAVE NARRATIVES

TYPEWRITTEN RECORDS PREPARED BY
THE FEDERAL WRITERS' PROJECT
1936-1938
ASSEMBLED BY

THE LIBRARY OF CONGRESS PROJECT
WORK PROJECTS ADMINISTRATION
FOR THE DISTRICT OF COLUMBIA
SPONSORED BY THE LIBRARY OF CONGRESS
WASHINGTON 1941

VOLUME XVII

VIRGINIA NARRATIVES

Prepared by
the Federal Writers' Project of
the Works Progress Administration
for the State of Virginia

HISTORIC PUBLISHING
All Rights Reserved
San Antonio, Texas
©2017

VIRGINIA SLAVE NARRATIVES

PREPARED FOR PUBLICATION BY
HISTORIC PUBLISHING
San Antonio, Texas
©2017

VIRGINIA SLAVE NARRATIVES

VIRGINIA SLAVE NARRATIVES

Slave Narratives: A Folk History of Slavery in the United States,
From Interviews with Former Slaves: Virginia Interviews

HISTORIC PUBLISHING
SAN ANTONIO, TEXAS
©2017

Transcriber's Notes:

To reflect the individual character of this document, most inconsistencies in spelling, punctuation, and formatting have been retained. Obvious typos and some punctuation (mostly quotation marks) have been fixed. Spelling changes are underlined in the text with a dotted line: original text appears in a mouse hoverbox over each corrected word, like this. All strike-outs over words were hand-written.

[HW: text] denotes hand-written addition unless otherwise noted.
[TR: text] denotes transcriber's note.

INFORMANTS

Berry, Fannie
Crawley, Charles

Fulkes, Minnie

Giwbs (Gibbs?), Georgina
Goodwin, Candis
Grandy, Charles
Harris, Della
Hines, Marriah
Hopson, Moble
Jones, Albert
Kelly, Susan, and Stokes, Simon
Slaughter, Richard
Sparks, Elizabeth
Wilson, Mary Jane

VIRGINIA SLAVE NARRATIVES

450009

Interview of Mrs. Fannie Berry, Ex-slave
861 E. Bank Street—Petersburg, Virginia
By Susie Byrd, Petersburg, Virginia

Date—February 26, 1937

NAT TURNER

Back 'fore the sixties, I can 'member my Mistress, Miss Sara Ann, comin' to de window an' hollerin', "De niggers is arisin'! De niggers is arisin'! De niggers is killin' all de white folks, killin' all de babies in de cradle!" It must have been Nat Turner's Insurrection; which wuz sometime 'fo de breakin' of de Civil War.

I wuz waitin' on table in dinin' room an' dis day dey had finished eatin' early an' I wuz cleanin' off table. Don't you know I must have been a good size gal.

JOHN BROWN

Yes, I 'member something 'bout him too. I know my Master came home an' said, dat on his way to de gallows ole John stopped an' kissed a little nigger child. "How com' I don't 'member? Don't tell me I don't 'cause I do. I don't care if its done bin a thousand years." I know what Master said an' it is as fresh in my mind as it wuz dat day. Dis is de song I herd my Master sing:

Old John Brown came to Harpers Ferry Town,

Purpose to raise an insurrection;

13

Old Governor Wise put the specks upon his eyes

An' showed him the happy land of Canaan.

INVENTION

My Master tole us dat de niggers started the railroad, an' dat a nigger lookin' at a boilin' coffee pot on a stove one day got the idea dat he could cause it to run by putting wheels on it. Dis nigger being a blacksmith put his thoughts into action by makin' wheels an' put coffee on it, an' by some kinder means he made it run an' the idea wuz stole from him an' dey built de steamengine.

RELATIONSHIP

I wuz one slave dat de poor white man had his match. See Miss Sue? Dese here ol' white men said, "what I can't do by fair means I'll do by foul." One tried to throw me, but he couldn't. We tusseled an' knocked over chairs an' when I got a grip I scratched his face all to pieces; an dar wuz no more bothering Fannie from him; but oh, honey, some slaves would be beat up so, when dey resisted, an' sometimes if you'll 'belled de overseer would kill yo'. Us Colored women had to go through a plenty, I tell you.

MARRIAGE

Elder Williams married me in Miss Delia Mann's (white) parlor on de crater road. The house still stands. The house wuz full of Colored people. Miss Sue Jones an' Miss Molley Clark (white), waited on me. Dey took de lamps an' we walked up to de preacher.

14

One waiter joined my han' an' one my husband's han'. After marriage de white folks give me a 'ception; an', honey, talkin' 'bout a table—hit wuz stretched clean 'cross de dinin' room. We had everythin' to eat you could call for. No, didn't have no common eats. We could sing in dar, an' dance ol' squar' dance all us choosed, ha! ha! ha! Lord! Lord! I can see dem gals now on dat flo'; jes skippin' an' a trottin'. An' honey, dar wuz no white folks to set down an' eat 'fo yo'.

WAR

Now, Miss Sue, take up. I jes' like to talk to you, honey 'bout dem days ob slavery; 'cause you look like you wan'ta hear all 'bout 'em. All 'bout de ol' rebels; an' dem niggers who left wid de Yankees an' were sat free, but, poor things, dey had no place to go after dey got freed. Baby, all us wuz helpless an' ain't had nothin'.

I wuz free a long time 'fo' I knew it. My Mistess still hired me out, 'til one day in talkin' to de woman she hired me to, she, "God bless her soul", she told me, "Fannie yo' are free, an' I don't have to pay your Master for you now." You stay with me. She didn't give me no money, but let me stay there an' work for vitals an' clothes 'cause I ain't had no where to go. Jesus, Jesus, God help us! Um, Um, Um! You Chillun don't know. I didn't say nothin' when she wuz tellin' me, but done 'cided to leave her an' go back to the white folks dat fus own me.

I plan' to 'tend a big dance. Let me see, I think it wuz on a Thursday night. Some how it tooken got out, you know how gals will talk an' it got to ol' Bil Duffeys ears (ol' dog!) an', baby do you know, mind you 'twont slavery time, but de 'oman got so mad cause I runned away from her dat she get a whole passel of 'em out looking for me. Dar wuz a boy, who heard 'em talkin' an' sayin' dey wuz goin' to kill me if I were found. I will never forget dis boy com' up to me while I wuz dancin' wid another man an' sed, "nobody knowes where you ar', Miss Moore, dey is lookin' fer you, an' is gwine kill you, so yo' come on wid me." Have mercy, have mercy my Lord, honey, you kin jes 'magin' my feelin' fer a minute. I couldn't move. You know de gals an' boys all got 'round me an' told me to go wid Squreball, dat he would show me de way to my old Mistess house. Out we took, an' we ran one straight mile up de road, den through de woods, den we had to go through a straw field. Dat field seem' like three miles. After den, we met another skit of woods. Miss Sue, baby my eyes, (ha! ha! ha!) wuz bucked an' too if it is setch a thin' as being so scared yo' hair stand on yo' head, I know, mine did. An' dat wasn't all, dat boy an' me puffed an' sweated like bulls. Was feared to stop, cause we might have been tracked.

At last we neared de house an' I started throwin' rocks on de porch. Child I look an' heard dat white 'oman when she hit dat floor, bouncin' out dat bed she mus' felt dat I wuz comin' back to her. She called all de men an' had 'em throw a rope to me an' day drawed me up a piece to de window, den I held my arms up an' dey snatched me in. Honey, Squreball fled to de woods. I ain't never heard nothin' 'bout him. An' do you know, I didn't leave day 'oman's house no more for fifteen years?

Lord! Lord! honey, Squreball an' I use to sing dis song.

> 'Twas 1861, the Yankees made de Rebels run
>
> We'll all go stone blin'
>
> When de Johny's come a marchin' home.

16

Child an' here's another one we use to sing. 'Member de war done bin when we would sing dese songs. Listen now:

> Ain't no more blowin' of dat fo' day horn
>
> I will sing, brethern, I will sing.
>
> A col' frosty mornin' de nigger's mighty good
>
> Take your ax upon your shoulder.
>
> Nigger talk to de woods,
>
> Ain't no mor' blowin' of dat fo' day horn.
>
> I will sing brethern, I will sing.

SONG

> Kemo, Kimo, dar you are
>
> Heh, ho rump to pume did'dle.
>
> Set back pinkey wink,
>
> Come Tom Nippecat
>
> Sing song Kitty cat, can't
>
> You carry me o'er?

<u>2</u>

Up de darkies, head so bold

Sing song, Kitty, can't you

Carry me O'er?

Sing Song, Kitty, can't yo'

Carry me home?

I wuz at Pamplin an' de Yankees an' Rebels were fightin' an' dey were wavin' the bloody flag an' a confederate soldier wuz upon a post an' they were shootin' terribly. Guns were firin' everywhere.

All a sudden dey struck up Yankee Doodle Song. A soldier came along [HW: and] called to me, "How far is it to the Rebels", an I honey, wuz feared to tell him. So, I said, "I don't know". He called me again. Scared to death [HW: I was]. I recollect gittin' behind the house an' pointed in the direction. You see, ef de Rebels knew dat I told the soldier, they would have killed me.

These were the Union men goin' after Lee's army which had don' bin 'fore dem to Appomattox.

The Colored regiment came up behind an' when they saw the Colored regiment they put up the white flag. (Yo' 'member 'fo' dis red or bloody flag was up). Now, do you know why dey raised dat white flag? Well, honey, dat white flag wuz a token dat Lee, had surrendered. Glory! Glory! yes, child the Negroes are free, an' when they knew dat dey were free dey, Oh! Baby! began to sing:

> Mamy don't yo' cook no mo',
> Yo' ar' free, yo' ar' free.
> Rooster don't yo' crow no mo',
> Yo' ar' free, yo' ar' free.

18

Ol' hen, don't yo' lay no mo' eggs,
Yo' free, yo' free.

Sech rejoicing an' shoutin', you never he'rd in you' life.

Yes, I can recollect de blowin' up of the Crater. We had fled, but I do know 'bout the shellin' of Petersburg. We left Petersburg when de shellin' commenced an' went to Pamplin in box cars, gettin' out of de way. Dem were scared times too, cause you looked to be kilt any minute by stray bullets. Just before the shellin' of Petersburg, dey were sellin' niggers for little nothin' hardly.

Junius Broadie, a white man bought some niggers, but dey didn't stay slave long, cause de Yankees came an' set 'em free.

450003

Interview of Mr. Charles Crawley, Ex-slave
By—Susie Byrd—Petersburg, Virginia
Date—February 20, 1937

THE STORY OF CHARLES CRAWLEY, EX-SLAVE

God knows how old I am. All I know is I wuz born 'fore de war.

Yes, I wuz a slave an' belonged to a family of Allen's in Luenburg County, came here to dis Petersburg de second week of Lee's surrender.

My Marster and Mistess wuz good to me as well as all us slaves. Dey owned 'bout fifty head of colored people. All de work I did wuz to play an' drive cows, being only a boy worked around as chillun; doin' dis, an' dat, little things de white folks would call me to do.

Marster Allen, owned my Mother, an' sister too; we emigrant (emigrated) here, came to dis town of Petersburg after Lee's surrender, I mean you now de ending of de Civil War. My mother, sister, and I came on down de road in a box car, which stopped outside de outskirts; hit didn't go through de city. Yes, I know when de first railroads were built, de Norfolk and Western an' de Atlantic Coast Line, dey were run through Petersburg an' in dem days it wuz called de Southern.

Mis and Mars' Allen didn't want us to leave dat part of de Country to come to dis here place down de road, but we comed ourselves to make a home fo' ourselves. Well now, we worked here an' dar, wid dis here man an' dat man; O well, wid different people 'til we bought us selves a home an' paid for it. Mother died right here in dis here house; twelve years ago, dis comin' March 'leventh. I am yet livin' in dis same house, dat she an' us all labored an' worked fo' by de sweat of our brow, an' wid dese hands, Lord! Lord! Child dem days wuz some days. Lemme finish, baby, tellin' you 'bout dis house. De groun' wad bought from a lady (colored) name Sis Jackey, an' she wuz sometimes called in dem days de Mother of Harrison Street Baptis' Church. I reccon dis church is de ol'est one in Petersburg.

O, yes, honey, I can 'member when de Yankees came into dis town; dey broke in stores an' told all de niggers to go in an' git anything dey wanted.

When slaves ran away they were brought back to their Master and Mistess; when dey couldn't catch 'em they didn't bother, but let 'em go. Sometimes de slaves would go an' take up an' live at tother places; some of 'em lived in de woods off of takin' things, sech as hogs, corn, an' vegetables from other folks' farm. Well, if dese slaves was caught, dey were sold by their new masters to go down South. Dey tell me dem Masters down South wuz so mean to slaves dey would let 'em work dem cotton fields 'til dey fall dead wid hoes in dare hands, 'en would beat dem. I'm glad to say, we had good owners.

There was a auction block, I saw right here in Petersburg on the corner of Sycamore street and Bank street. Slaves were auctioned off to de highest bidder. Some refused to be sold. By dat I mean, "cried". Lord! Lord! I done seen dem young'uns fought and kick like crazy folks; child it wuz pitiful to see 'em. Den dey would handcuff an' beat 'em unmerciful. I don' like to talk 'bout back dar. It brun' a sad feelin' up me. If slaves 'belled, I done seed dem whip 'em wid a strop cal' "cat nine tails." Honey, dis strop wuz 'bout broad as yo' hand, from thum' to little finger, an' 'twas

21

cut in strips up. Yo' done seen dese whips dat they whip horses wid? Well dey was used too.

You sed somethin' 'bout how we served God. Um, um, child, I tell you jest how we use to do. We use to worship at different houses. You see you would git a remit to go to dese places. You would have to show your remit. If de Pattyrollers, caught you dey would whip yo'. Dats de wa' dey done in dem da's. Pattyrollers, is a gang of white men gitting together goin' through de country catching slaves, an' whipping an' beatin' 'em up if dey had no remit. Marster Allen wouldn't 'llow no one to whip an' beat his slaves, an' he would handle anybody if dey did; so, Marster's slaves met an' worshipped from house to house, an honey, we talked to my God all us wanted.

You know we use to call Marster Allen, Colonel Allen. His name was Robert. He was a home general, an' a lawyer, too. When he went to court any slave he said to free, was freed an' turned aloose. De white fo'ks as well as slaves obeyed Marster Allen.

Did you know poor whites like slaves had to git a pass? I mean, a remit like as slaves, to sell anythin' an' to go places, or do anythin'. Jest as we colored people, dey had to go to some big white man like Colonel Allen, dey did. If Marster wanted to, he would give dem a remit or pass; an' if he didn't feel like it, he wouldn't do it. It was jes as he felt 'bout hit. Dats what made all feared him. Ol' Marster was more hard on dem poor white folks den he was on us niggers.

I don't know but two sets of white folks slaves up my way; one was name Chatman, an' de tother one Nellovies. Dese two families worked on Allen's farm as we did. Off from us on a plot called Morgan's lot, there dey lived as slaves jes like us Colored fo'ks. Yes de poor white man had some dark an' tough days, like us poor niggers; I mean were lashed an' treated, some of 'em, jes as pitiful an' unmerciful. Lord! Lord! baby, I hope yo' young fo'ks will never know what slavery is, an' will never suffer as yo' foreparents. O God! God! I'm livin' to tell de tale to yo', honey. Yes, Jesus, yo've spared me.

For clothin' we were 'lowed two suits a year—one fer spring, an' one fer winter, was all yo' had. De underclothes were made at home. Yo' also got two pairs of shoes an' homemade hats an' caps. The white folks or your slave owners would teach dem who could catch on easy an' dey would teach de other slaves, an' dats how dey kept all slaves clothed. Our summer hats were made out of plaited straw, underclothes made out of sacks an' bags.

We had plenty of food such as 'twas—cornbread, butter milk, sweet potatoes, in week days. Ha! Ha! honey, guess dat's why niggers don't like cornbread today; dey got a dislike for dat bread from back folks. On Sunday we had biscuits, and sometimes a little extra food, which ole Mistess would send out to Mother for us.

Fer as I think, if slavery had lasted, it would have been pretty tough. As it was, some fared good, while others fared common. You know, slaves who were beat an' treated bad; some of dem had started gittin' together an' killin' de white folks when dey carried dem out to de field to work. God is punishin' some of dem ol' suckers an' their chillun right now fer de way dey use to treat us poor colored fo'ks.

I think by Negro gittin' educated he has profited, an' dis here younger generation is gwine to take nothin' off dese here poor white folks when dey don't treat dem right, cause now dis country is a free country; no slavery now.

450013

Interview of Mrs. Minnie Fulkes
459 E. Byrne Street—Petersburg, Virginia
By—Susie Byrd
March 5, 1937

I was born the twenty-fifth of December and I am 77 years old. My mother was a slave and she belonged to Dick Belcher in Chesterfield County. Old Dick sold us again to Gelaspe Graves. 'Member now fifteen of mother's chillun went with her having de same master.

Honey, I don't like to talk 'bout dem times, 'cause my mother did suffer misery. You know dar was an' overseer who use to tie mother up in de barn with a rope aroun' her arms up over her head, while she stood on a block. Soon as dey got her tied, dis block was moved an' her feet dangled, yo' know—couldn't tech de flo'.

Dis ol' man, now, would start beatin' her nekkid 'til the blood run down her back to her heels. I took an' seed th' whelps an' scars fer my own self wid dese here two eyes. (this whip she said, was a whip like dey use to use on horses); it wuz a piece of leather 'bout as wide as my han' from little finger to thumb. After dey had beat my muma all dey wanted another overseer. Lord, Lord, I hate white people and de flood waters gwine drown some mo. Well honey dis man would bathe her in salt and water. Don't you kno' dem places was a hurtin'. Um, um.

I asked mother what she done fer 'en to beat and do her so? She said, nothin', tother than she refused to be wife to dis man.

An' muma say, if he didn't treat her dis way a dozen times, it wasn't nary one.

Mind you, now muma's marster didn't know dis wuz going on. You know, if slaves would tell, why dem overseers would kill 'em.

An' she sed dat dey use to have meetings an' sing and pray an' th' ol' paddy rollers would hear dem, so to keep th' sound from goin' out, slaves would put a great big iron pot at the door, an' you know some times dey would fer git to put ol' pot dar an' the paddy rollers would come an' horse whip every las' one of 'em, jes cause poor souls were praying to God to free 'em from dat awful bondage.

Ha! ha! ha! dar wuz one ol' brudder who studied fer 'em one day an' tol all de slaves how to git even wid 'em.

He tol' 'em to tie grape vines an' other vines across th' road, den when de Paddy rollers come galantin' wid their horses runnin' so fast you see dem vines would tangle 'em up an' cause th' horses to stumble and fall. An' lots of times, badly dey would break dere legs and horses too; one interval one ol' poor devil got tangled so an' de horse kept a carryin' him, 'til he fell off horse and next day a sucker was found in road whar dem vines wuz wind aroun' his neck so many times yes had choked him, dey said, "He totely dead." Serve him right 'cause dem ol' white folks treated us so mean.

Well, sometimes, you know dey would, the others of 'em, keep going 'til dey fin' whar dis meeting wuz gwine on. Dey would come in and start whippin' an' beatin' the slaves unmerciful. All dis wuz done to keep yo' from servin' God, an' do you know some of dem devils wuz mean an' sinful 'nough to say, "Ef I ketch you here agin servin' God I'll beat you. You haven't time to serve God. We bought you to serve us." Um, um.

God's gwine 'rod dem wicket marsters. Ef hit 'taint 'em whut gits hit, hits gonna fall on deir chillun.

25

In dem back days child, meetings wuz carried on jes like we do today, somewhatly. Only difference is the slave dat knowed th' most 'bout de Bible would tell and explain what God had told him in a vision (yo' young folks say, "dream") dat dis freedom would come to pass; an' den dey prayed fer dis vision to come to pass, an' dars whar de paddy rollers would whip 'em ag'in.

Lord! Lord dey, pew! pew! pew! Baby, I jes kno' I could if I knowed how to write, an' had a little learning I could put off a book on dis here situation. Yo' kno what I mean 'bout dese way back questions yo' is a asking me to tell yo' 'bout; as fer as I can recallect in my mind.

When Graves bought us, he sold three of us an' three slaves. My brother an' sister went down south. Muma sed to de cotton country an' too, she say, "they were made to work in th' cotton fields by their new marster, out in dem white fields in th' brawlin' sun from th' time it breaked day 'till yo' couldn't see at night an', yes indeedy, an' if God isn't my right'ous judge they were given not half to eat, no not 'nough, to eat. Dey wuz beaten ef dey ask'd for any mo'".

As to marriage, when a slave wanted to marry, why he would jes ask his marster to go over and ask de tother marster could he take unto himself dis certain gal fer a wife. Mind you now, all de slaves dat marster called out of quarters an' he'd make 'em line up see, stand in a row like soldiers, and de slave man is wid his marster when dis askin' is gwine on, and he pulls de gal to him he wants; an' de marster den make both jump over broom stick an' after dey does, dey is prenounced man an' wife, both stayin' wid same marsters (I mean ef John marries Sallie, John stay wid his ol' marster an' Sal' wid hers, but had privileges, you know, like married folks; an' ef chillun were born all of 'em, no matter how many, belonged to de marster whar de woman stayed).

If I aint made a mistake, I think it wuz in April when de war surrendered an' muma an' all us wuz turned aloose in May. Yes dat ol' wench, a ol' heifer, oh child, it makes my blood bile when I think 'bout it. Yes she kept muma ig'runt. Didn't tell her nuthing 'bout being free 'til den in May.

Den her mistess, Miss Betsy Godsey, tol' her she wuz free, an' she (muma) coul' cook fer her jes th' same dat she would give her something to eat an' help clothe us chillun, dat wuz ef muma continual' to sta wid her an' work.

You see, we didn't have nuthin' an' no whar to go, um, um, um so we all, you know, jes took en stayed 'til we wuz able wid God's help to pull us selves together. But my God it wuz 'ginst our will, but, baby, couldn't help ourselves.

My fathers master tol' him he could farm one half fer th' tother an' when time rolled 'roun' fer dem 'viding crops he took an' give to him his part like any honest man would do. Ah, Lord child, dem wuz terrible times too, oh! it makes me shudder when I think of some slaves had to stay in de woods an' git long best way dey could after freedom done bin' clared; you see slaves who had mean master would rather be dar den whar dey lived. By an' by God opened a way an' dey got wid other slaves who had huts. You see, after th' render no white folks could keep slaves. Do yo' know even now, honey, an' dat done bin way bac' yonder, dese ol' white folks think us poor colored people is made to work an' slave fer dem, look! dey aint give you no wages worth nuthin'. Gal cook all week fer two an' three dollars. How can you live off it, how kin, how kin yo'?

My father waited on soldiers and after de s'render dey carried him an' his brother as fer as Washington D.C. I think we all use to say den, "Washington City." Aint you done heard folks talk 'bout dat city? 'Tis a grade big city, daus whar de President of dis here

27

country stay; an' in bac' days it wuz known as 'vidin' lin' fer de North an' South. I done hear dem white folks tell all 'bout dem things—dis line. As I wuz tellin' you, his brother wuz kept, but dey sent father bac' home. Uncle Spencer wuz left in Prince Williams County. All his chillun ar' still dar. I don't know de name of Yankee who carried him off.

Lord, Lord, Honey, dem times too over sad, 'cause Yankees took lots of slaves away an' dey made homes. An' whole heap of families lost sight of each other. I know of a case whar after hit wuz ten years a brother an' sister lived side by side an' didn't know dey wuz blood kin.

My views 'bout de chillun in dem bac' days is dat dese here chillun what is now comin' up is too pizen brazen fer me.

No jes' lem me tell you how I did I married when I wuz 14 years old. So help me God, I didn't know what marriage meant. I had an idea when you loved de man, you an' he could be married an' his wife had to cook, clean up, wash, an' iron fer him was all. I slept in bed he on his side an' I on mine fer

Den muma said "Come here chillun," and she began tellin' me to please my husband, an' 'twas my duty as a wife, dat he had married a pu'fect lady.

Dese here chillun don't think of deir principle. Run purfectly wild. Old women too. Dey ain't all 'em true to one, but have two.

Jes what is gittin' into dis generation; is hit de worl' comin' to an end?

Ha! ha! ha! I goin' tel' yo' som'thin' else.

I had a young man to come to see me one evenin' an' he sed dis to me, "Miss Moore" "Let me jin my fence to your plantation."

I give him his hat. I say, "no" yo' go yo' way an' I go mine. I wuz through wid him, an' mind yo' I from dat da' 'til dis aint knowed what he wuz talkin' 'bout an' wuz ashamed to ask muma; but I thought he insulted me.

I didn't never go to school. Had to work an' am working now an' when hit breaks good weather, I go fishing. And who works dat big garden out dar? No body but me.

You know I'm mother of eleven chillun', an' 'tis seven living an' four of dem ded.

450014 Duplicate—Copy #1

Interview of Mrs. Georgina Giwbs, Ex-slave
By—Thelma Dunston
Portsmouth, Virginia
January 15, 1937

Mrs. Georgina Giwbs, an ex-slave, resides at 707 Lindsey Avenue, Portsmouth, Virginia. The old lady marveled at the great change that has been made in the clothings, habits and living conditions of the Negro since she was a child. She described the clothing of the slaves in a calm manner, "All of de cloth during slavery time was made on de loom. My mastah had three slaves who worked in de loom house. After de cloth was made, mastah sent hit over town to a white woman who made hit in clothes. We had to knit all our stockings and gloves. We'd plait blades of wheat to make us bonnets. We had to wear wooden bottom shoes. Dere won't no stores, so we growed everything we et, an' we'd make everything we'd wear."

"We had a washing house. Dere wuz five women who done de washing an' ironing. Dey had to make de soap. Dat wuz done by letting water drip over oak ashes. Dis made oak ash lye, and dis wuz used in making soap. After de clothes had soaked in dis lye-soap and water, dey put de clothes on tables and beat 'em 'till dey wuz white."

"Mastah give us huts to live in. De beds wuz made of long boards dat wuz nailed to de wall. De mattress wuz stuffed wif straw and pine tags. De only light we had wuz from de fire-place. We didn't use no matches, 'stead we'd strick a rock on a piece of steel. We'd let the sparks fall on some cotton."

"My mastah had 'bout five hundred slaves. He'd never sell none of his slaves, but he'd always buy more. Dat keeps de slaves from marrying in dere famblies. When yer married, yer had to jump over a broom three times. Dat wuz de licence. Ef mastah seen two slaves together too much he would marry them. Hit didn't make no difference ef yer won't but fourteen years old."

"Work began at sun rise and last 'till sun down. When I wuz eight years old, I started working in de field wif two paddles to keep de crows from eatin' de crops. We had a half day off on Sunday, but you won't 'lowed to visit. Sometimes de men slaves would put logs in de beds, and dey'd cover 'em up, den dey go out. Mastah would see de logs and think dey wuz de slaves."

"My father told me dere wuz once a mastah who sold a slave woman and her son. Many years after dis, de woman married. One day when she wuz washing her husband's back she seen a scar on his back. De woman 'membered de scar. It wuz de scar her mastah had put on her son. 'Course dey didn't stay married, but de woman wouldn't ever let her son leave her."

Superstitions told by Mrs. Georgina Giwbs

1. "Ef a dog turns on his back and howls', 'tis a sign of death."

2. "Ef yer drops a dish rag on de floor and it spreads out, 'tis de sign dat a hungry woman is gwine ter come to yer house. Ef de rag don't spread out den a hungry man is a coming."

3. "Ef a black cat crosses yer path going to de right, 'tis good luck. Ef de cat goes to de left 'tis bad luck."

4. "Ef a girl walks aroung wif one shoe off and one on, she'll stay single as many years as de number of steps she taken."

450006
Interview of Mrs. Candis Goodwin
Aged 80
Cape Charles, Virginia

Ah ain't knowd, 'xactly, how ol' ah is, but ah bawn 'fo' de war. Bawn ovuh yonder at Seaview, on ol' Masser Scott's plantation. Tain't fur f'om here. Yes, reckon ah 'bout six yeah ol' when de Yankees come, jes' a lil' thin', you know.

My white people dey good tuh me. Cose dey gits mad wid you but dey don' beat non o' us; jes' ack lak it. Why, ah was jes lak dey's chullun; ah played wid 'em, et wid 'em an' eb'n slep' wid 'em. Ah kinder chillish, ah reckon. Had muh own way. Muh mommer, she wuck in de quater kitchen. She ain' ha' tuh wuck hawd lak some. Had it kinder easy, too. Jes' lak ah tells yuh ah al'ys had my way. Ah gits whut ah wants an' ef'n dey don't gi' tuh me, ah jes' teks it.

No neber had no wuck to do in dem days 'ceptin' nursin' de babies. 'Twas jes' lak play; twan no wuck. Uster go ober to Nottingham's tuh play, go long wid Missus chillun, yuh know. Ah laks tuh go ober there cause dey has good jam an' biscuits. Ef'n dey don gi' me none, ah jes' teks some. Dey don do nuttin'; jes' say, "Tek yuh han' out dat plate". But ah got whut ah wants den. Why we chillun user hab a time 'round ol' Missus' place. All us chillun uster git togeder an' go in de woods tuh play. Yes, de white and black uns, too. De grea' big whi' boys uster go 'long wid us, too. Know how we play? We tek de brown pine shadows an' mek houses outer 'em an' den mek grass outer de green uns. Den we go ober Missus' dairy and steal inything we want an' tek it to our houses in de woods. Dem was good ol' times, ah tel yuh, honey.

Tel yuh, whut ah uster do. Ah uster play pranks on ol' Masser Scott. Ah's regular lil' devil, ah was. Come night, ev'y body sit 'round big fire place in living room. Soon it git kinder late, Massa git up outer his cheer tuh win' up, de clock. Ah gits hin' his cheer ret easy, an' quick sneak his cheer f'om un'er him; an' when he finish he set smack on de flow! Den he say "Dogone yuh lil' cattin', ah gwan switch yuh!" Ah jes' fly out de room. Wont sceered though cause ah knows Massa won' gon do nottin' 'tuh me.

What ah know 'bout whippin'. Well ah ain' had uh whippin' in my life. But ah hear tel o' how dey whips um though. Yuh know dey uster tek dat cowhide an' cut 'em till dey backs beeds. Some jes' lak see de blood run down. Better not cry neider. Mek yuh holler, "Oh pray! oh pray!" Couldn't say nottin' else. But Massa Scott neber had none dat kinder stuff on his place. He say tain't right. Didn't 'low no paddyrollers 'round eider. Say dey "trechous". Massa Nottin'ham neber had 'em on his place neider. He didn' neber strike one o' his niggers; nobody else better not neider.

Honey, ah teh yuh ah growd jes' as good's any chil' in dis country. Ol' Missus Scott gimme good clothes; cose ah didn't git 'em mone twice a yeah, but dey's good when ah gits 'em. She gimmie Sis' dresses. Sis' one ob Missus' little girls. An' de whi' chillun dey learn me how tuh read, too. Cose de whi' folks din wan' yuh to learn. Ah 'member jes' as clare as yestidy how one dem chillun learn me how tuh read "compress-i-bility". Thought ah was suppin' den! Ah kin read Bible lil now but ah can' write; neber learn tuh write.

Did ah eber go tuh church? Cose ah did! Went ret 'long wid Missus' chillun. Had tuh set in de back, but dat won' nottin'. My mommer, she went tuh church too. Sometime de ol' folk uster git togedder in de quater-kitchen tuh shout an' pray. Dats where my mommer git 'ligion. She kinder tender 'oman; couldn' stan' dat preachin' no longer.

What 'bout muh pappy? Dat's suppin' ah ain' tol' yuh 'bout. Well, yuh know Uncle Stephen, he kinder overseer fo' some widow 'omans. He Mommer husband. He come see muh mommer any time he gits ready. But ah fin' out he ain' muh pappy. Ah knowd dat since when ah's a lil' thin'. Ah uster go ovur tuh massa William's plantation. Dey tell me all 'bout. De folks ober dere dey uster say tuh me, "Who's yuh pappy? Who's yuh pappy?" Ah jes' say "Tuckey buzzard lay me an' de sun hatch me" an' den gwan 'bout my business. Cose all de time dey knows an' ah knows too dat Massa Williams was muh pappy. Ah tell yuh suppin' else. Got uh brother libin' ret on dis here street; one den toof doctors, yuh know, what pulls yer teef. Cose he's white. But tain't knowed 'roun' here. 'Twould ruin him. He's a nice man though. Uster go tuh see muh son an' his wife, lots uh times. Yes dey's good frien's.

Yes, dey had overseers. Sometime dey call dem stewards. Had colored uns too. Massa Scott had white overseers, good man though; but Massa Nottin'ham, he had big black boss on his place. [HW illegible over: ~~cain'~~] 'member his name. He ain' had to git no p'mission tuh come tuh our place. He jes' come an' goes when he gits ready.

Kin ah 'member de war? Yes, indeed! 'Member jes' lak 'twas yestidy. Well dey had a stow down de conner f'om Massa's plantation, an' dey al'ys sen' me tuh stow fo' tuh buy things. Uster go down dere, an' dem Yankees be sittin' all 'long de road wid dey blue coats; ret pretty site; 'twas. But ah's sceard tuh deaf, when ah gits neah 'em. Ah gits what ah wants f'om de stow, an' flys pass 'em. Dem Yankees show had dey way. Dey went in all de white folks house; tek dey silver, an' inything dey big 'nough carry out. Jes' ruin Missus furniture; get up on de table an' jes' cut capper.

34

Nasty things! Den de Yankees goes 'round at night, tek anybody dey wants tuh help 'em fight. Twas dey "Civil right". Got my Jake, cose ah neber knowd him den. He twelve yeah oller ah is.

Lemmie tell yuh 'bout muh Jake, how he did in de war. He big man in dey war. He drill soldiers ev'y day. Firs' he be in one dem companies—Company "C" ah bliebe. Den he wucked up to be sergent-Major, in de Tenth Regiment. Jacob [HW illegible over: Godium] his name was. He say all look up tuh him an' 'spect him too. See dat "Sowd" ov'in dat coner? Dat's de ve'y sowd he used in de war, an' ah kep' it all dese yeahs. No de soldiers neber did no fighting 'round here's ah know of. But plenty ob 'em camped here.

My Jake, he hansome man, he was. 'Member, how we firs' got togeder. We all was tuh church one Sunday, an' Jake he kep' cidin' up to me. An' ah lookin' at him outer de coner muh eye, till finally he come up an' took holt muh han's. 'Twas aft' de war ah had growd up. Ah was in muh early teens den. Dey say ah's de purtiet girl on de Shore. An' when Jake an' me got married, ev'ybody said, "You show maks a purty couple."

De ol' Scott chillun what ah growd up wid? No, mone dem lef' now. Dey las' girl died heah las' yeah an' hur daughter come way down here f'om up in Maryland tuh tell "An' Candis" 'bout it. Wouldn' tell me sceard 'twould 'cite me. But ah hea'd hur tellin' my chil dere all 'bout it. Ol' Massa Scott's chillun, some dem, dey still comes tuh see me. Slip me some money now'n den, an' suppin' t'eat, too. Dey's all moughty nice folks, dem Scotts is.

450011

Interview of Mr. Charles Grandy, Ex-slave
By—David Hoggard
Date—February 26, 1937
[HW: Norfolk, Va.]

History of Ex-slave and Civil War Veteran

Charles Grandy was born February 19, 1842, in Mississippi. While still an infant, he was brought to Norfolk. When the family arrived in Norfolk his father was arrested on some pretentious charge, and the whole family was placed in prison. After their release, they were taken to a plantation near Hickory Ground, Virginia, and sold. Slaves, at this time, were often taken to rural districts in carts, and sold to owners of plantations, as they were needed. Family life, friendships, and love affairs were often broken up; many times never to be united.

Following the general routine of slaves, the Grandy family was given a shanty; food and clothing was also issued to them, and had to last until the master decided to give out another supply. Usually, he issued them their allowance of food weekly. Often the supply was insufficient for their needs.

Charles played around the plantation "big house", doing small errands until he reached the age of five, then his play days ended. While playing on the wood pile one morning, his master called him, "boy do you see this grass growing along the side of the fence? Well pull it all up." When his first task was finished, he was carried to the field to pull the grass from the young cotton and other growing crops. This work was done by hand because he was still too young to use the farm implements. Now he went to his task daily; from early in the morning until late in the evening. The long toilsome days completely exhausted the youngster. Often he would fall asleep before reaching home and spend a good portion of the night on the bare ground. Awakening, he would find it quite a problem to locate his home in the darkness of night.

From the stage of grass pulling by hand, he grew strong enough, in a few years, to use the hoe rake and sickle. While attempting to carry out his master's orders to cut corn tassels with a large sharp knife, his elbow was seriously cut. He was taken to the house and treated, the application being chimney soot, to stop the bleeding. After this treatment the arm was placed in a sling, and eventually became deformed from insufficient care. He was sent back to the fields to pick cotton, with one free hand and his teeth, while painfully carrying the other hand in the sling. Failing to obey this command, he would have been given a whipping, or sent to the southlands. Sending slaves to the plantations of Mississippi and other southern states was a type of punishment all slaves feared.

Slaves were not allowed much freedom of worship. The Yankee soldiers and officers played a great part in the slave's moral training, and religious worship. They secretly instructed small gatherings of slaves, at night. The points stressed most were, obedience and the evils of stealing. There were some sections where masters were liberal in their views toward their slaves, and permitted them to worship openly.

Slaves were allowed to have small quantities of whiskey, even during the days of their worship, to use for medicinal purposes. It was a common occurrence to see whiskey being sold at the foot of the hill near the churchyard.

The news of war, and the possibility of Negroes enlisting as soldiers was truly a step closer to the answering of their prayers for freedom. Upon hearing of this good news Grandy joined a few of the others in this break for freedom. One night, he and a close friend packed a small quantity of food in a cloth and set out about midnight to join the northern army. Traveling at night most of the time, they were constantly confronted with the danger of being recaptured. Successfully eluding their followers, they reached Portsmouth after many narrow escapes. From Portsmouth they moved to Norfolk. Arriving in Norfolk, Grandy and his friend decided to take different roads of travel. Several days and nights found him wandering about the outskirts of Norfolk, feeding on wild berries, etc. While picking berries along a ditch bank, he was hailed by a Yankee soldier, who having come in contact with run away slaves before, greeted him friendly, and questioned him of his home and of his knowledge of work. He was taken to camp and assigned as cook. At first, he was not very successful in his job, but gradually improvement was shown. He was asked what wages he would accept. It was such a pleasure to know that he had escaped the clutches of slavery, he did not ask for wages; but instead, he was willing to work for anything they would give him, no matter how small, as long as he didn't have to return to slavery.

Within a short period he was given a uniform and gun; was fully enlisted as a soldier, in the 19th regiment of Wisconsin, Company E. Here he remained in service until November, 1862, after which time he returned to Norfolk to spend some time with his mother, who was still living. While sitting in the doorway one day, with his Mother, he was again confronted with the proposition of reenlisting. He agreed to do so for one year, to serve as guard at Fortress Monroe. He remained there until the close of the War, offering brave and faithful services.

Mr. Grandy is now ninety-five years old, residing at 609 Smith Street, Norfolk, Virginia. He is still able to attend the various conventions of Civil War Veterans. He can read, write, and has a fair knowledge of the Bible. His main interest is the organization of Negroes into strong groups. He enjoys talking about religion and is quite an interesting and intelligent person to talk with.

450005

Interview of Mrs. Della Harris
2 E. Byrne Street
Petersburg, Virginia
By—Susie Byrd
February 5, 1937

"I don't know just how old I is. Muma sent me to private school wid white chillun fo' one week. I was 13 years old at de time uh Lee's surrender. I belong to Peter or Billy Buck Turnbull Warrenton, N.C. <u>Put this down.</u> My mother and family all belong to Peter Buck as his slaves. We didn't work until after the war; then we came to Petersburg. I went to dancing school wid the white folks and can dance any kind of dance sets. My father was a musicianer. He belonged to John Carthan, in Warrenton, N.C. In dem days you had to take your Moster's and Mistess' name. In slavery time when a slave married he had to ask his Moster and Mistess.

"We never went to church. We used to hear de bells ringing loud, baby, yes, clear and strong. No, never seen [HW: no] Sunday school, and the first time I went in a church I looked all around, and baby, I thought dat I was in heaven. It wasn't long, Miss Sue, before I got 'ligeon, and, yes, I jined [HW: de] church, 15 years old I wuz. Never will forget the time, or dat place. Den I lived here with an ant, muma's sister, who was named Kate Williams. Her husband wuz my uncle, and he worked and died at de White House in Washington City.

"I don't know de name of de President he worked for, but you can find dat out on dem books. You know you young folks calls um records.

39

"Yes child I'm proud of my age never gave no body no trouble.

"I have 8 children dead and now only one son living. Peter Turnbull was good to all his slaves, as far as I know. Mama was a cook in slavery time. She died in Petersburg, yes, right here in dis hole.

"No muma never owned any thing, always rented and aint never owned nothing but a passel of children.

"My muma was a genuine Indian. Some people say you can't own Indians. I don't know how cum, but I do know she was owned by these people, but she surely was an Indian. Every body knows me all over Virginia.

"When I use to be in dining room service I would hear de white folks talk, and, do you know, Miss Sue you can hear a lot that way?

"Moster said he couldn't sell me 'cause I was so little. Just kept me fur to wait on de little chillun in de house.

"Miss Sue, you'll have to give me something for telling you all dis here, if it ain nothing but a horse cake.

"I've seen lots of dis world in travel. Done bin to Baltimore City; done bin to Philidelphia.

"I aint gwine give you no more, gal.

"Yes, to Lynchburg, den I worked at Mont Royal School, Baby, where Mrs McDaniel was manager.

"The man gwine say, 'dat woman bin some where.' If I stayed long enough I mighta got some learning but I stayed only one year.

40

Got tired of that place. From one season to another is a year, aint it? Ah! Lord!

"Young folks now adays are just fur a good time, and a good time too they have. Yes, Siree Bob!

"Gwine stop now, Miss Sue, aint gwine give you no mo'. Man gwine say, Miss Sue, where in the devil did you get this stuff? Gal, you are a mess. You gonna write most all dat book about Della. Go on now, dats nough.

"In dem days chillun were chillun, now every body is grown. Chillun then were seen and not heard. When old persons came around muma sent us out and you better not be seen. Now every body [HW: act] grown. Make the man laugh.

"I've always enjoyed good health. Never had a Doctor in my life, not even when my chillun wuz born. Dis rubbing when people got pain just rubs it in. Eating so much and late hours is cause you young folks dying. All muma's chillun wuz healthy.

"[HW: Real] food in dem days, yes, muma fed us good vituals from white folks. I tell you, we had good owners. I didn't see sun set when I wuz a child. Always went to bed early, child, I wish I could call back dem days. Muma said people lived so much longer because they took care of themselves.

"All dis here education an' people just now got it."

[HW: Question:] Do you think, Mrs. Harris, education has helped our race?

"Well, child, I don' know. Folks are so indifferent now I am afraid to say. Pshaw.... Colored folks now. Some are messy [HW: an'] don't know how to be polite.

"Talking about lightning days. Its lightning at every bodys house. Lord have mercy on dese here young folks and deliber me from the plantation, I pray.

"Courting dem days wuz like everything I reckon you all do now adays. You promise to 'bey the man, but before you finish its cussing, Honey.

"In olden days husbands loved. Sho God did tend to wife and took care of them and they had to stay home cause it wuz always a new baby. I tell you, Miss Sue, man ought not never had you to find history 'cause you gwine tell it all. As I said, we loved. Is de young folks marrying fur love? Dey don't stay together long enough to warm hands. We went to church together and praised God; led prayer meetings and, yes siree, would feel good.

"Now you all done start opening theatres on Sunday. Miss Sue, all dat stuff you putting down will sure make the man laugh."

450004

Interview of Mrs. Marriah Hines
E. Avenue R.F.D. 1.
Oakwood Norfolk, Virginia
By—David Hoggard
March 26, 1937

Mrs. Marriah Hines—Born July 4, 1835, South Hampton County Virginia, a slave on James Pressmans plantation. Now residing on E. Avenue, Oakwood, Norfolk, Virginia R.F.D. 1.

[HW: Insert last paragraph] [TR: appropriate paragraph inserted here] Marriah is about four feet and a half tall and weighs about one hundred pounds. She has a pretty head of white hair covering her round brown face. Her memory of her mother and father is very vague, due to their death when she was young. She is able to dress herself practically without help, and to get about from place to place alone, enjoying talking about religion and [HW: what she knows about] the world [HW: of] today.

Even though the general course of slavery was cruel, Marriah Hines was fortunate enough, not to have to endure its severities. James Pressman was one of the few slave masters that looked upon the slave with a certain degree of compassion, to whom Marriah was fortunate, to be owned by. Although slavery in its self was cruel; but the fact that Mr. Pressman was generous and kind to the slaves that he owned, because of necessity in the process of his farming, should not be overlooked. It is quite true that slave masters near him did not grant their slaves such priviliges as he did. I do not wish to impress the idea that Mr. Pressman did not approve of slavery, but only his general attitude toward his slaves was different from the majority of the slaves holders. From the following story of Marriah's life in slavery, it may be clearly seen that her master was an exception.

Upon interviewing her, she relates her life story as follows

"I lived with good people, my white folks treated us good. There was plenty of 'em that didn't fare as we did. Some of the poor folks almost starved to death. Why the way their masters treated them was scandalous, treated them like cats and dogs. We always had plenty of food, never knowed what it was to want food bad enough to have to steal it like a whole lot of 'em. Master would always give us plenty when he give us our rations. Of course we slaves were given food and clothing and just enough to keep us goin good. Why master would buy cloth by the loads and heaps, shoes by the big box full; den he'd call us to the house and give each on 'us our share. Plenty to keep us comfortable, course it warn't silk nor satin, no ways the best there was, but 'twas plenty good 'nough for us, and we was plenty glad to git it. When we would look and see how the slaves on the 'jining farm was fareing, 'twould almost make us shed tears. It made us feel like we was gitting 'long most fine. Dat's why we loved 'spected master; 'course he was so good to us.

"'Cause master was good and kind to us, some of the other white folks used to call him 'nigger lover.' He didn't pay dat no mind though. He was a true Christian man, and I mean he sho' lived up to it. He never did force any of us to go to church, if we didn't want to, dat was left to us to 'cide. If you wanted to you could, if you didn't you didn't have to, but he'd always tell us, you ought to go.

"Not only was master good but his whole family was too. When the weather was good we worked in the fields and on other little odd jobs that was needed done. We slaves would eat our breakfast, and go to the fields, dare wont no hurry-scurry. Lots o'times when we got in the fields the other slaves had been in the field a long time. Dar was times though we had to git to it early, too, 'pecially if it had been rainy weather and the work had been held up for a day or so. Master didn't make us work a 'tall in bad weather neither when it got real cold. The men might have to git in fire wood or sumpin' of that sort but no all day work in the cold— just little odd jobs. We didn't even have to work on Sundays not even in the house. The master and the preacher both said dat was the Lord's day and you won't spose to work on that day. So we didn't. We'd cook the white folks victuals on Saturday and lots o'times dey eat cold victuals on Sundays. Master would sometimes ask the preacher home to dinner. 'You plenty welcome to go home with me for dinner, but you'll have to eat cold victuals 'cause there aint no cooking on Sundays at my house.' Lots of times we slaves would take turns on helping 'em serve Sunday meals just 'cause we liked them so much. We hated to see Missie fumbling 'round in the kitchen all out 'a'her place. We didn't have to do it, we just did it on our own free will. Master sometimes gives us a little money for it too, which made it all the better. Master and Missus was so good to us we didn't mind working a little on Sundays, in the house. Master had prayer with the whole family every night, prayed for us slaves too. Any of the slaves that wanted to jine him could. Or if they wanted to pray by dem selves they could. Sundays we went to church and stayed the biggest portion of the day. No body had to rush home. On our plantation we had general prayer meeting every Wednesday night at church. 'Cause some of the masters didn't like the way we slaves carried on we would turn pots down, and tubs to keep the sound from going out. Den we would have a good time, shouting singing and praying just like we pleased. The paddarollers didn't pay us much 'tention coused they knew how master let us do. Dey would say nasty things 'bout master 'cause he let us do like we did.

"We had plenty time to ourselves. Most of the time we spent singing and praying 'cause master was sich a good Christian and most of us had 'fessed religion. Evenings we would spin on the old spinning wheel, quilt make clothes, talk, tell jokes, and a few had learned to weave a little bit from Missus. We would have candy pulls, from cooked molasses, and sing in the moonlight by the tune of an old banjo picker. Chillen was mostly seen, not heard, different from youngens of today talking backward and foward cross their mammies and pappies. Chillen dat did dat den would git de breath slapped out on 'em. Your mammies didn't have to do it either; any old person would, and send you home to git another lickin'. We slaves had two hours off for dinner, when we could go home and eat before we finished work 'bout sun down. We aint had no colored overseers to whip us nor no white ones. We just went 'long so and did what we had to, wid out no body watching over us. Every body was just plum crazy 'bout master. Doing the day you could see him strutting down the field like a big turkey gobbler to see how the work was going on. Always had a smile and a joke wid you. He allu's tell us we was doing fine, even sometimes when we want. We'd always catch up our work, so he wouldn't have to fuss. We loved Misses and the chillen so much we wouldn't even let 'em eat hardly. Missus didn't have to do nothing, hardly. Dare was always some of us round the house.

"'Bout a year fore we heard 'bout freedom, master took sick and the slaves wouldn't'er looked sadder if one of their own youngens had been sick. Dey 'spected him to die, and he kept calling for some cabbage. Misses finally let me cook him some cabbage, and let him have some 'pot licker' (the water the cabbage was cooked in). He didn't die den but a few years later he did die. Dat was the first and the last time any cooking ever was done in that house on Sunday.

"When master told us we was free it didn't take much 'fect on us. He told us we could go where we pleased and come when we pleased that we didn't have to work for him any more 'less we wanted to. Most of us slaves stayed right there and raised our own crops. Master helped us much as he could. Some of us he gave a cow or a mule or anything he could spare to help us. Some of us worked on the same plantation and bought our own little farms and little log cabins, and lived right there till master dies and the family moved away. Some of us lived there right on. Master married me to one of the best colored men in the world, Benjamin F. Hines. I had five chullun by him, four girls and one boy, two of the girls and the boy are dead. Dey died 'bout 1932 or 33. I stay with one awhile, den I go and stay awhile wid the other one.

"We didn't have no public schools in dem days 'n time. What little learning you got it from the white chillen."

450012

[HW: Terms and phrasing to be checked and verified in further interviews.]

THE STORY OF "UNCLE" MOBLE HOPSON.
(pronounced Mobile)

Interview Saturday, November 28th at his home on the Poquoson River.
(Recorded from memory within 1 hour after "being talked to by him.")

47

Uncle Moble hobbles unsteadily from his little shade beside the outhouse into the warm kitchen, leaning heavily on the arm of his niece. He looks up on hearing my voice, and extends a gnarled and tobacco-stained hand. He sinks fumblingly into a chair. It is then that I see that Uncle Moble is blind.

"No, don't mind effen yuh ast me questions. Try tuh answer 'em, I will, best ways I kin. Don't mind et all, effen yuh tell me whut yuh want to know. Born'd in fifty-two, I was, yessuh, right here over theer wheer dat grade big elum tree usta be. Mammy was uh Injun an' muh pappy was uh white man, least-ways he warn't no slave even effen he was sorta dark-skinned.

"Ole pappy tole me 'bout how cum the whites an' the blacks an' the Injuns get all mixed up. Way back 'long in dere it war, he nevuh tell me jes' what year, dey was a tribe uh Injuns livin 'long dis ribber. Dey was kin to de Kink-ko-tans, but dey wasn't de same. Dey had ober on the James de Kink-ko-tans an' dey had dis tribe ober here.

"Well, de white man come. Not fum ober dere. De white man cum cross de Potomac, an' [HW: den he] cross de York ribber, an' den he cum on cross de Poquoson ribber into dis place. My pappy tell me jes' how cum dey cross all uh dose ribbers. He ain't see it, yuh unnerstan, but he hear tell how et happen.

"Dis whut de white man do. He pick hisself a tall ellum long side de ribber an' he clumb to de top an' he mark out on de trunk wid he ax uh section 'long 'bout, oh, 'long 'bout thirty-fo'ty feet. Den he cut de top off an' den he cut de bottom off so de thick trunk fall right on de edge uh de ribber. An' den he hollar out dat ellum log tell he make hisself uh bout an' he skin off de bark so et don't ketch in de weeds. Den he make hisse'f uh pattle an' dey all makes pattles an' dey floats dat boat an' pattles cross to de udder side.

48

"Well, dey cross de Potomac an' dey has tuh fight de Injuns an' dey cross de York an' fit some more tell dey kilt all de Injuns or run 'em way. When dey cross de Poquoson dey fine de Injuns ain't aimin' tuh fight but dey kilt de men an' tek de Injun women fo' dey wives. Coursen dey warn't no marryin' dem at dat time.

"Well dat's how cum my people started. Ah hear tell on how dey hafta fight de Injuns now an den, an' den de Britishers come an' dey fit de British.

"An' all uh dat time dere warn't no black blood mixed in 'em, least wise, not as I heer'd tell uh any. Plenty blacks 'round; ah seen 'em. My pappy nevuh would have none. My oncle had 'em, ober on dat pasture land dere was his land.

"Why I usta get right out dere many uh day and watch 'em at workn' [HW: in de 'baccy fields.] Big fellars dey was, wid cole-black skins ashinin' wid sweat jes' lak dey rub hog-fat ober dere faces. Ah ain't nevuh bothered 'em but my bruther—he daid now sence ninety-three he got uh hidin' one day fo' goin' in de field wid de blacks.

[HW: Insert] "Well we all heer tell uh de was, [HW: an ah listen to de grown folk talk on et,] but dey ain't paid so much mind to et. Tell one day de blacks out in de field an' dey ain't no one out dere tuh mek 'em work. An' dey stand 'round an' laugh an' dey get down an' wait, but dey don' leave dat field all de mawning. An' den de word cum dat de Yankees was a comin,' an' all dem blacks start tuh hoopin' an' holl'rin', an' den dey go on down to deer shacks an' dey don' do no work at all dat day.

"An' when do Yanks [HW: git heer] dey ain't non uh de slave-holders no whers round. Dey all cleared out an' de blacks is singin' an' prayin' an' shoutin' fo' joy cause Marse Lincoln done set em free.

"Well, dey tuk de blacks an' dey march em down de turnpike to Hampton, an' den dey put em tuh work at de fort. Ah ain't nevuh go ober dere but ah heer tell how de blacks come dere fum all 'round tell dey git so many dey ain't got work fo' 'em tuh do, so dey put 'em tuh pilin' up logs an' teking 'em down agin, an' de Yankees come and go an' new ones come but dey ain't troublin nothin' much 'ceptin' tuh poach uh hawg or turkey now an' den.

"Ah was jes' a little shaver gittin' in my teens den but ah 'member clear as day all ah dat. An' ah heer tell uh uh big battle up Bethel way an' dey say dey kilt up dere uh bunch uh men, de 'federates an' de Yankees both. But ah ain't seed it, though Oncle Shep Brown done tole me all 'bout et.

"Oncle Shep Brown lived down aways on de ribber. 'Long 'fore de Yankees come he jined up wid de 'federates. He fit in dat battle at Big Bethel but he ain't get uh scratch. He tell me all 'bout de war when he come back home. He tell me all 'bout de fall uh Richmond, he did.

"Was one day down [HW: en] de lower woods in de shade he tell me 'bout Richmond, Oncle Shep did. Why, I remember et jes' lak it was yestiddy. Was whittlin' uh stick, he was, settin' on uh stump wid his game laig hunched up ontuh uh bent saplin'. He was whittlin' away fo' uh 'long time 'thout sayin' much, an' all at once he jump in de air an' de saplin' sprang up an he start in tuh cussin.

"'Gawdammit, gawdammit, gawdammit,' he kept sayin' tuh hisse'f an' limpin' round on dat laig game wid de roomatissum. Ah know he gonna tell me sompin den cause when Oncle Shep git ehcited he always got uh lot tuh say.

"'Gawdammit,' he say, 'twas de niggahs tak Richmond.'

"'How dey do dat Oncle Shep?' ah ast, though ah knowed he was gonna tell me anyway.

"'De niggahs done tuk Richmond,' he keep on sayin' an' finally he tell me how dey tak Richmond.

"'Ah seed et muhse'f,' he say, 'my comp'ny was stationed on de turnpike close tuh Richmond. We was in uh ole warehouse,' he told me, 'wid de winders an' de doors all barred up an' packed wid terbaccy bales awaitin' fo' dem Yanks tuh come. An' we was a-listenin' an' peepin' out an' we been waitin' dere most all de ev'nin'. An' den we heer [HW: uh] whistlin' an' uh roarin' like uh big blow an' it kep' gittin' closer. But we couldn't see nothin' uh comin' de night was so dark. ~~But~~ Dat roarin' kep' a-gittin' louder an' louder an' 'long 'bout day break there cum fum down de pike sech uh shoutin' an uh yellin' as nevuh in muh born days ah'd heerd.'

"'An' de men in dat warehouse kept askinkin' away in de darkness widdout sayin' nothin', cause dey didn't know what debbils de Yankees was alettin' loose. But ah stayed right there wid

51

dem dat had de courage tuh face et, cause ah know big noise mean uh little storm.'

"'Dar was 'bout forty of us left in dat ole warehouse ahidin' back of dem bales uh cotton an terbaccy, an' peepin out thew da cracks.'

"'An' den dey come. Down de street dey come—a shoutin' an' aprancin' an' a yellin' an' asingin' an' makin' such uh noise like as ef all hell done been turn't loose. Uh [HW: mob uh] nigguhs. Ah ain't nevuh knowed nigguhs—even all uh dem nigguhs—could mek sech uh ruckus. One huge sea uh black faces filt de streets fum wall tuh wall, an' dey wan't nothin' but nigguhs in sight.'

"'Well, suh, dey warn't no usen us firin' on dem cause dey ain't no way we gonna kill all uh dem nigguhs. An pretty soon dey bus' in de do' uh dat warehouse, an' we stood dere whilst dey pranced 'rounst us a hoopin' an' holl'rin' an' not techin' us at all tell de Yankees soljers cum up, an' tek away our guns, an' mek us prisoners an' perty soon dey march us intuh town an' lock us up in ole Libby Prison.'

"'Thousings of 'em—dem nigguhs.' he say, 'Yassir—was de nigguhs dat tuk Richmond. Time de Yankees get dere de nigguhs done had got de city tuk.'"

[HW: **II**]
[HW: **<u>Why Uncle Moble is a Negro</u>**]

Uncle Moble is a noble figure. He turns his head toward me at my questions, just as straight as if he actually is looking at me.

"Yuh wanta know why I'm put with the colored people? [HW: Sure, ah got white skin, leastwise, was white las' time ah' see et.] Well, ah ain't white an' ah ain't black, leastwise not so fur as ah know. 'Twas the war done that. Fo de war dere warn't no question come up 'bout et. Ain't been no schools 'round here tuh bothuh 'bout. Blacks work in de fields, an' de whites own de fields. Dis land here, been owned by de Hopson's sence de fust Hopson cum here, I guess, back fo' de British war, fo' de Injun war, ah reck'n. Ustuh go tuh de church school wid ole Shep Brown's chillun, sat on de same bench, ah did.

"But de war changed all dat. Arter de soljers come back home, it was diff'runt. First dey say dat all whut ain't white, is black. An' [HW: den] dey tell de Injuns yuh kain't marry no more de whites. An' den dey tell usen dat we kain't cum no more tuh church school. An' dey won't let us do no bisness wid de whites, so we is th'own in wid de blacks.

"Some [HW: uh our folk] moved away, but dey warn't no use uh movin' cause ah hear tell et be de same ev'y wheer. So perty soon et come time tuh marry, an' dey ain't no white woman fo' me tuh marry so ah marries uh black woman. An' dat make me black, ah 'spose 'cause ah ben livin' black ev'y sence.

"But mah bruther couldn't fine no black woman dat suited him, ah reckon, cause he married his fust cousin, who was a Hopson huhse'f.

"Den dere only chile married hisse'f uh Hopson, and Hopsons been marryin' Hopsons ev'y sence, ah reck'n."

Uncle Moble Tells Where to Dig A Well

"That well out dere? Naw, dat ain't old. Dat ain't been dere mo'un fifteen-twenty year. De ole well, she was ole, though she nevuh war much good. Paw ain't dug et in de right place. Old Shep

Brown tolt him, but my old man ain't nevuh pay no mine to old Shep.

"But old Shep sho' did know how tuh dig uh well. Ah kin see now him ah comin' up de lane when paw was adiggin'. Moble he say—my paw an' me had de same name—Moble, ye ain't diggin' dat well de right place.

"'Diggin' et wheer ah wants et,' answers paw, a diggin' away en de hole shoulder deep.

"'Well, ye ain't gonna git much water. Oughta got yo'se'f uh ellum stick.'

"'Don' need no ellum stick. Diggin' dis well in my own youd an' ah'm gonna dig et jes' wheer ah wants et. Go haid an' dig yo' own well.'

"Well, old Shep musta got sorta mad, cause he goes home an' de nex' day he digs hisse'f uh well.

"Ah seen him. Ah watched him when he figgered wheer tuh dig dat well. Sho' nuf old Shep got hisse'f uh prime ellum stick fum ah good sized branch dat was forked. First he skint all de bark off.

"'Kain't fine no water lessen ye skin de bark off,' he tell me. Long 'bout 2-3 feet on each limb, et was. Well, old Shep tek dat ellum stick wid one fork in each hand an' de big end straight up in de air an' he holt it tight an' started tuh walk around, wid me followin' right on his heels. An sho' nuff, perty soon ah seed dat branch commence tuh shake an' den et started tuh bend an' old Shep let et lead him across de field wid et bendin' lower all de time tell perty soon de big end uh dat ellum stick point straight down.

"Old Shep marked de spot an' got his pick an' commence tuh dig out dat spot. An' fo' old Shep had got down mo'un five uh six feet ah be dawg ef he don' hit uh stream uh water dat filt up de well in uh hurry so dat he git his laigs all wet fo' he kin clamb out.

"An' yuh moughten believe et but ah know dat tuh be uh fac', cause ah tuk dat ellum stick in muh own han's an' ah felt dat stick apullin' me back tuh dat water. No matter which way ah turn, dat stick keep atwistin' me roun' toward dat water. An' ah tried tuh pull et back an' old Shep tuk hole uh et wid me an' tried tuh hole et up straight but de big end uh dat ellum branch pult down and pointed tuh dat well spite uh both uh us.

"Still dere? Nawsuh, ah reckon dat old well been crumbled in an' filled up long time now. Old Shep died back en 93, ah reckon. His old shack blowed down, an' ah reckon dat ole well all covered up. But dat was some well while she lasted. Gave mo' water dan all de udder wells in Poquoson, ah reckon."

450008

[HW: **Jones, Albert**]

**Interview of Ex-slave and
Civil War Veteran
Portsmouth, Virginia
By—Thelma Dunston
January 8, 1937**

Civil War Veteran of Portsmouth, Virginia

On the outskirts of Portsmouth, Virginia, where one seldom hears of or goes for sightseeing lives Mr. Albert Jones. In a four room cottage at 726 Lindsey Avenue, the aged Civil War Veteran lives alone with the care of Mr. Jones' niece, who resides next door to him. He has managed to survive his ninety-fifth year. It is almost a miracle to see a man at his age as suple as he.

On entering a scanty room in the small house, Mr. Jones was nodding in a chair near the stove. When asked about his early life, he straightened up ~~on his spine~~, crossed his legs and said, "I's perty old—ninety six. I was born a slave in Souf Hampton county, but my mastah wuz mighty good to me. He won't ruff; dat is 'f yer done right."

The aged man cleared his throat and chuckled. Then he said, "But you better never let mastah catch yer wif a book or paper, and yer couldn't praise God so he could hear yer. If yer done dem things, he sho' would beat yer. 'Course he wuz good to me, 'cause I never done none of 'em. My work won't hard neiver. I had to wait on my mastah, open de gates fer him, drive de wagon and tend de horses. I was sort of a house boy."

"Fer twenty years I stayed wif mastah, and I didn't try to run away. When I wuz twenty one, me and one of my brothers run away to fight wif the Yankees. Us left Souf Hampton county and went to Petersburg. Dere we got some food. Den us went to Fort Hatton where we met some more slaves who had done run away. When we got in Fort Hatton, us had to cross a bridge to git to de Yankees. De rebels had torn de bridge down. We all got together and builded back de bridge, and we went on to de Yankees. Dey give us food and clothes."

The old man then got up and emptied his mouth of the tobacco juice, scratched his bald head and continued. "Yer know, I was one of de first colored cavalry soljers, and I fought in Company 'K'. I fought for three years and a half. Sometimes I slept out doors, and sometimes I slept in a tent. De Yankees always give us plenty of blankets."

"During the war some uh us had to always stay up nights and watch fer de rebels. Plenty of nights I has watched, but de rebels never 'tacked us when I wuz on."

"Not only wuz dere men slaves dat run to de Yankees, but some uh de women slaves followed dere husbands. Dey use to help by washing and cooking."

"One day when I wuz fighting, de rebels shot at me, and dey sent a bullet through my hand. I wuz lucky not to be kilt. Look. See how my hand is?"

The old man held up his right hand, and it was half closed. Due to the wound he received in the war, that was as far as he could open his hand.

Still looking at his hand Mr. Jones said, "But dat didn't stop me, I had it bandaged and kept on fighting."

"The uniform dat I wore wuz blue wif brass buttons; a blue cape, lined wif red flannel, black leather boots and a blue cap. I rode on a bay color horse—fact every body in Company 'K' had bay color horses. I tooked my knap-sack and blankets on de horse back. In my knap-sack I had water, hard tacks and other food."

"When de war ended, I goes back to my mastah and he treated me like his brother. Guess he wuz scared of me 'cause I had so much ammunition on me. My brother, who went wif me to de Yankees, caught rheumatism doing de war. He died after de war ended."

W11805 [TR: moved from bottom of page]

Writer—Jayne, Lucille B.
Capahosic, Virginia.
Gloucester Co.
Typist—Nicholas

[HW: C. Moore]
[HW: Tales]
[HW: Virginia/1938-9]

FOLKLORE

Material from Upper Guinea.

In the upper part of Guinea, generally known as the "Hook," you will find two very interesting characters, both Negroes. Aunt Susan Kelly, who is a hundred years old, and Simon Stokes, who is near a hundred.

Aunt Susan is loved by all who know her, for she is a very lovable old Negro.

Aunt Susan's Story

"My mammy, Anna Burrell, was a slave, her massa wuz Col. Hayes, of Woodwell; he wuz very good ter his slaves. He nebber sold mammy or us chilluns; he kept we alls tergether, and we libed in a little cabin in de yard.

"My job wuz mindin' massa's and missus' chilluns all dey long, and puttin' dem ter baid at night; dey had ter habe a story told ter dem befo' dey would go ter sleep; and de baby hed ter be

59

rocked; and I had ter sing fo' her 'Rock a-by baby, close dem eyes, befo' old san man comes, rock a-by baby don' let old san man cotch yo' peepin',' befo' she would go ter sleep.

"Mammy used ter bake ash-cakes; dey wuz made wid meal, wid a little salt and mixed wid water; den mammy would rake up de ashes in de fire-place; den she would make up de meal in round cakes, and put dem on de hot bricks ter bake; wen dey hed cooked roun' de edges, she would put ashes on de top ob dem, and wen dey wuz nice and brown she took dem out and washed dem off wid water.

"Mammy said it wuz very bad luck ter meet a woman early in de mornin' walkin'; and nebber carry back salt dat yo' habe borrowed, fo' it will bring bad luck ter yo' and ter de one yo' brung it ter. If yo' nose iches on de right side a man is comin', if de lef' side iches a woman is comin'; if it iches on de end a man and woman is sho' ter come in a short.

"For a hawk ter fly ober de house is sho' sign ob death, fo' de hawk will call corpses wen he flies ober."

Simon Stokes, son of Kit and Anna Stokes, is quite a type. He and his parents with his brothers and sisters were slaves; owned by George W. Billups, of Mathews County, who later moved to Gloucester County and bought a farm near Gloucester Point. They had eleven children, Simon is the only one living.

Simon's Story

"Massa George and missus wuz good ter his slaves. My mammy wuz missus' cook; and him and de odder boys on de farm worked in de co'n and de terbaccer and cotton fields.

"Me sho' didn't lik dat job, pickin' worms off de terbaccer plants; fo' our oberseer wuz de meanes old hound you'se eber seen, he hed hawk eyes fer seein' de worms on de terbaccer, so yo' sho' hed ter git dem all, or you'd habe ter bite all de worms dat yo' miss into, or git three lashes on yo' back wid his old lash, and dat wuz powful bad, wusser dan bittin' de worms, fer yo' could bite right smart quick, and dat wuz all dat dar wuz ter it; but dem lashes done last a pow'ful long time.

"Me sho' did like ter git behind de ox-team in de co'n field, fo' I could sing and holler all de day, 'Gee thar Buck, whoa thar Peter, git off dat air co'n, what's de matter wid yo' Buck, can't yo hear, gee thar Buck.'

"In de fall wen de simmons wuz ripe, me and de odder boys sho' had a big time possum huntin', we alls would git two or three a night; and we alls would put dem up and feed dem hoe-cake and simmons ter git dem nice and fat; den my mammy would roast dem wid sweet taters round them. Dey wuz sho' good, all roasted nice and brown wid de sweet taters in de graby.

"We alls believed dat it wuz bad luck ter turn back if yer started anywher, if yo' did bad luck would sho' foller yer; but ter turn yo' luck, go back and make a cross in yo' path and spit in it."

450001

Autobiography of Richard Slaughter

(Given by himself as an oral account during an interview between himself and writer, December 27,1936.) Claude W. Anderson—Hampton, Virginia

"Come in, son. Have a seat, who are you and how are you? My life? Oh! certainly you don't want to hear that! Well, son, have you been born again? Do you know Christ? Well, that's good. Good for you. Amen. I'm glad to hear it. Always glad to talk to any true Christian liver. God bless you, son.

"I was born January 9, 1849 on the James at a place called Epps Island, City Point. I was born a slave. How old am I! Well, there's the date. Count it up for yourself. My owner's name was Dr. Richard S. Epps. I stayed there until I was around thirteen or fourteen years old when I came to Hampton.

"I don't know much about the meanness of slavery. There was so many degrees in slavery, and I belonged to a very nice man. He never sold but one man, fur's I can remember, and that was cousin Ben. Sold him South. Yes. My master was a nice old man. He ain't living now. Dr. Epps died and his son wrote me my age. I got it upstairs in a letter now.

"It happened this a-way. Hampton was already burnt when I came here. I came to Hampton in June 1862. The Yankees burned Hampton and the fleet went up the James River. My father and mother and cousins went aboard the Meritanza with me. You see, my father and three or four men left in the darkness first and got aboard. The gun boats would fire on the towns and plantations and run the white folks off. After that they would carry all the colored folks back down here to Old Point and put 'em behind the Union lines. I know the names of all the gunboats that came up the river.

Yessir. There was the Galena, we called her the old cheese box, the Delware, the Yankee, the Mosker, and the Meritanza which was the ship I was board of. That same year the Merrimac and Monitor fought off Newport News Point. No, I didn't see it. I didn't come down all the way on the gunboat. I had the measles on the Meritanza and was put off at Harrison's Landing. When McCellan retreated from Richmond through the peninsula to Washington, I came to Hampton as a government water boy.

"While I was aboard the gunboat, she captured a rebel gunboat at a place called Drury's Bluff. When I first came to Hampton, there were only barracks where the Institute is; when I returned General Armstrong had done rite smart.

"I left Hampton still working as a water boy and went to Quire Creek, Bell Plains, Va., a place near Harper's Ferry. I left the creek aboard a steamer, the General Hooker, and went to Alexandria, Va. Abraham Lincoln came aboard the steamer and we carried him to Mt. Vernon, George Washington's old home. What did he look like? Why, he looked more like an old preacher than anything I know. Heh! Heh! Heh! Have you ever seen any pictures of him? Well, if you seen a picture of him, you seen him. He's just like the picture.

"You say you think I speak very good English. Heh! Heh! Heh! Well, son I ought to. I been everywhere. No I never went to what you would call school except to school as a soldier. I went to Baltimore in 1864 and enlisted. I was about 17 years old then. My officers' names were Capt. Joe Reed, Lieutenant Stimson, and Colonel Joseph E. Perkins. I was assigned to the Nineteenth Regiment of Maryland Company B. While I was in training, they fought at Petersburg. I went to the regiment in '64 and stayed in until '67. I was a cook. They taken Richmond the fifth day of April 1865. On that day I walked up the road in Richmond.

"When we left Richmond, my brigade was ordered to Brownsville, Texas. We went there by way of Old Point Comfort, where we went aboard a transport. When we got to Brownsville, I was detailed to a hospital staff. We arrived in Brownsville in January 1867. The only thing that happened in Brownsville while I was there was the hanging of three Mexicans for the murder of an aide. In September we left Brownsville and came back to Baltimore. Before we left I was sent up the Rio Grande to Ringo Barracks as boss cook.

"I then returned to Hampton and lived as an oysterman and fisherman for over forty years.

"I have never been wounded. My clothes have been cut off me by bullets but the Lord kept them off my back, I guess.

"I tell you what I did once. My cousin and I went down to the shore once. The river shore, you know, up where I was born. While we were walking along catching tadpoles, mimows, and anything we could catch, I happened to see a big moccasin snake hanging in a sumac bush just a swinging his head back and forth. I swung at 'im with a stick and he swelled his head all up big and rared back. Then I hit 'im and knocked him on the ground flat. His belly was very big so we kept hittin' 'im on it until he opened his mouth and a catfish as long as my arm (forearm), jumped out jest a flopping. Well the catfish had a big belly too, so we beat 'em on his belly until he opened his mouth and out came one of these women's snapper pocketbooks. You know the kind that closes by a snap at the top. Well the pocket book was swelling all out, so we opened it, and guess what was in it? Two big copper pennies. I gave my cousin one and I took one. Now you mayn't believe that, but it's true. I been trying to make people believe that for near fifty years. You can put it in the book or not, jest as you please, but it's true. That fish swallowed some woman's pocketbook and that snake just swallowed him. I have told men that for years and they wouldn't believe me.

"While I was away my father died in Hampton. He waited on an officer. My mother lived in Hampton and saw me married in 1874. I bought a lot on Union Street for a hundred dollars cash. I reared a nephew, gave him the lot and the house I built on it an he threw it away. When I moved around here, I paid cash for this home.

"Did slaves ever run away! Lord yes, all the time. Where I was born, there is a lots of water. Why there used to be as high as ten and twelve Dutch three masters in the habor at a time. I used to catch little snakes and other things like terapins and sell 'em to the sailor for to eat roaches on the ships. In those days a good captain would hide a slave way up in the top sail and carry him out of Virginia to New York and Boston.

"I never went in the Spanish American War. Too old, but I had some cousins that enlisted. That was during McKinley's time. He went down the Texas and some of them other ships they gave Puerto Rico Hail Columbia. They blew up the Maine with a mine. She was blowed up inward. The Maine left Hampton Roads going towards Savannah. When they looked at what was left of her all the steel was bent inward which shows that she was blowed up from the outside in. Understand. During the World War I went to Washington and haven't been anyplace since. I'm a little hard of hearing and have high blood pressure. So I have to sit most of the time. Got an invitation in there now wantin' me to come to a grand reunion of Yankees and the Rebels this year but I can't go. Getting too old. Well goodbye, son. Glad to have you come again sometime."

450010

Autobiography of Elizabeth Sparks

(Interviewed at Matthews Court House, Virginia January 13, 1937. By Claude W. Anderson.)

Come in boys. Sure am glad ter see ya. You're lookin' so well. That's whut I say. Fight boys! Hold em! You're doin' alright. Me, I'm so mean nothin' can hurt me. What's that! You want me to tell yer 'bout slavery days. Well I kin tell yer, but I ain't. S'all past now; so I say let 'er rest 's too awful to tell anyway. Yer're too young to know all that talk anyway. Well I'll tell yer some to put in yer book, but I ain'ta goin' tell yer the worse.

My mistress's name was Miss Jennie Brown. No, I guess I'd better not tell yer. Done forgot about dat. Oh well, I'll tell yer. Some, I guess. She died 'bout four years ago. Bless her. She 'uz a good woman. Course I mean she'd slap an' beat yer once in a while but she warn't no woman fur fighting fussin' an' beatin' yer all day lak some I know. She was too young when da war ended fur that. Course no white folks perfect. Her parents a little rough. Whut dat? Kin I tell yer about her parents? Lord yes! I wasn't born then but my parents told me. But I ain't a goin' tell yer nuffin. No I ain't. Tain't no sense fur yer ta know 'bout all those mean white folks. Dey all daid now. They meany good I reckon. Leastways most of 'em got salvation on their death beds.

Well I'll tell yer some, but I ain'ta goin' tell yer much more. No sir. Shep Miller was my master. His ol' father, he was a tough one. Lord! I've seen 'im kill 'em. He'd git the meanest overseers to put over 'em. Why I member time after he was dead when I'd peep in the closet an' jes' see his old clothes hangin' there an' jes' fly.

Yessir, I'd run from them clothes an' I was jes' a little girl then. He wuz that way with them black folks. Is he in heaven! No, he ain't in heaven! Went past heaven. He was clerk an' was he tough! Sometimes he beat 'em until they couldn't work. Give 'em more work than they could do. They'd git beatin' if they didn't get work done. Bought my mother, a little girl, when he was married. She wuz a real Christian an' he respected her a little. Didn't beat her so much. Course he beat her once in a while. Shep Miller was terrible. There was no end to the beatin' I saw it wif my own eyes.

Beat women! Why sure he beat women. Beat woman jes' lak men. Beat women naked an' wash 'em down in brine. Some times they beat 'em so bad, they jes' couldn't stand it an' they run away to the woods. If yer git in the woods, they couldn't git yer. Yer could hide an' people slip yer somepin' to eat. Then he call yer every day. After while he tell one of colored foreman tell yer come on back. He ain'ta goin' beat yer anymore. They had colored foreman but they always have a white overseer. Foreman git yer to come back an' then he beat yer to death again.

They worked six days fum sun to sun. If they forcin' wheat or other crops, they start to work long 'fo day. Usual work day began when the horn blow an' stop when the horn blow. They git off jes' long 'nuf to eat at noon. Didn't have much to eat. They git some suet an' slice a bread fo' breakfas. Well, they give the colored people an allowance every week. Fo' dinner they'd eat ash cake baked on blade of a hoe.

I lived at Seaford then an' was roun' fifteen or sixteen when my mistress married. Shep Miller lived at Springdale. I 'member jes' as well when they gave me to Jennie. We wuz all in a room helpin' her dress. She was soon to be married, an' she turns 'roun an' sez to us. Which of yer niggers think I'm gonna git when I git married? We all say, "I doan know." An' she looks right at me an' point her finger at me like this an' sayed "yer!" I was so glad. I had to make 'er believe I 'us cryin', but I was glad to go with 'er. She didn't beat. She wuz jes' a young thing. Course she take a whack at me sometime, but that weren't nuffin'. Her mother wuz a mean ol' thin'. She'd beat yer with a broom or a leather strap or anythin' she'd git her hands on.

She uster make my aunt Caroline knit all day an' when she git so tired aftah dark that she'd git sleepy, she'd make 'er stan' up an knit. She work her so hard that she'd go to sleep standin' up an' every time her haid nod an' her knees sag, the lady'd come down across her haid with a switch. That wuz Miss Jennie's mother. She'd give the cook jes' so much meal to make bread fum an' effen she burnt it, she'd be scared to death cause they'd whup her. I 'member plenty of times the cook ask say, "Marsa please 'scuse dis bread, hits a little too brown." Yessir! Beat the devil out 'er if she burn dat bread.

I went wif Miss Jennie an' worked at house. I didn't have to cook. I got permission to git married. Yer always had to git permission. White folks 'ud give yer away. Yer jump cross a broom stick tergether an' yer wuz married. My husband lived on another plantation. I slep' in my mistress's room but I ain't slep' in any bed. Nosir! I slep' on a carpet, an' ole rug, befo' the fiahplace. I had to git permission to go to church, everybody did. We could set in the gallery at the white folks service in the mornin' an' in the evenin' the folk held baptize service in the gallery wif white present.

Shep went to war but not for long. We didn't see none of it, but the slaves knew what the war wuz 'bout. After the war they tried to fool the slaves 'bout freedom an' wanted to keep 'em on a workin' but the Yankees told 'em they wuz free. They sent some of the slaves to South Carolina, when the Yankees came near to keep the Yankees from gittin' 'em. Sent cousin James to South Carolina. I nevah will forget when the Yankees came through. They wuz takin' all the livestock an' all the men slaves back to Norfolk, wid 'em to break up the system. White folks head wuz jes' goin' to keep on havin' slaves. The slaves wanted freedom, but they's scared to tell the white folks so. Anyway the Yankees wuz givin' everythin' to the slaves. I kin heah 'em tellin' ol' Missy now. "Yes! give'er clothes. Let'er take anythin' she wants." They even took some of Miss Jennie's things an' offered 'em to me. I didn't take 'em tho' cause she'd been purty nice to me. Whut tickled me wuz my husban', John Sparks. He didn't want to leave me an' go cause he didn't know whah they's takin' 'em nor what they's gonna do, but he wanted to be free; so he played lame to keep fum goin'. He was jes' a limpin' 'round. It was all I could do to keep fum laffin'. I kin hear Miss Jennie now yellin' at them Yankees. No! who are yer to Judge. I'll be the judge. If John Sparks wants to stay here, he'll stay. They was gonna take 'im anyhow an' he went inside to pack an' the baby started cryin'. So one of 'em said that as long as he had a wife an' a baby that young they guess he could stay. They took all the horses, cows, and pigs and chickens an' anything they could use an' left. I was about nineteen when I married. I wuz married in 1861, my oldest boy was born in 1862 an' the fallin' of Richmond came in 1865.

Before Miss Jennie was married she was born an' lived at her old home right up the river heah. Yer kin see the place fum ou side heah. On the plantation my mother wuz a house woman. She had to wash white folks clothes all day an' huh's after dark. Sometimes she'd be washin' clothes way up 'round midnight. Nosir, couldn't wash any nigguh's clothes in daytime. My mother lived in a big one room log house wif an' upstairs. Sometimes the white folks give yer 'bout ten cents to spend. A woman with children 'ud git 'bout half bushel of meal a week; a childless woman 'ud git 'bout a peck an' a half of meal a week. If yer wuz workin', they'd give yer shoes. Children went barefooted, the yeah 'round. The men on the road got one cotton shirt an' jacket. I had five sisters an' five brothers. Might as well quit lookin' at me. I ain't gonna tell yer any more. Cain't tell yer all I know. Ol Shep might come back an' git me. Why if I was to tell yer the really bad things, some of dem daid white folks would come right up outen dere graves. Well, I'll tell somemore, but I cain't tell all.

Once in a while they was free nigguhs come fum somewhah. They could come see yer if yer was their folks. Nigguhs used to go way off in quarters an' slip an' have meetin's. They called it stealin' the meetin'. The children used to teach me to read. Schools! Son, there warn't no schools for niggers. Slaves went to bed when they didn't have anything to do. Most time they went to bed when they could. Sometimes the men had to shuck corn till eleven and twelve o'clock at night.

If you went out at night the paddyrols 'ud catch yer if yer was out aftah time without a pass. Mos' a the slaves was afeared to go out.

Plenty of slaves ran away. If they ketch 'em they beat 'em near to death. But yer know dey's good an' bad people every where. That's the way the white folks wuz. Some had hearts; some had gizzards 'stead o' hearts.

When my mothers's master died, he called my mother an' brother Major an' got religion an' talked so purty. He say he so sorry that he hadn't found the Lord before an' had nuttin' gainst his colored people. He was sorry an' scared, but confessed. My mother died twenty years since then at the age of seventy-fo'. She wuz very religious an' all white folks set store to 'er.

Old Massa done so much wrongness I couldn't tell yer all of it. Slave girl Betty Lilly always had good clothes an' all the priviliges.

She wuz a favorite of his'n. But cain't tell all! God's got all! We uster sing a song when he was shippin' the slaves to sell 'em 'bout "Massa's Gwyne Sell Us Termerrer." No, I cain't sing it for yer. My husban' lived on the plantation nex' to my mistress. He lived with a bachelor master. He tell us say once when he was a pickinnany ol' Marse Williams shot at 'im. He didn't shoot 'em; he jes' shoot in the air an' ol' man wuz so sceered he ran home an' got in his mammy's bed. Massa Williams uster play wif 'em; then dey got so bad that they'ud run an' grab 'is laige so's he couldn't hardly walk so when he sees 'em he jes' shoots in de air. Ol' Massa, he, jes' come on up ter the cabin an' say "mammy whah dat boy?" She say, in dah undah the bed. Yer done scared 'im to deaf! Ol' Massa go on in an' say, Boy! What's the mattah wid yer. Boy say, yer shot me master yer shot me! Master say, aw Gwan!—Git up an' come along. I ain't shot yer. I jes' shot an' scared yer. Heh! Heh! Heh! Yessir my ol' husban' sayed he sure was scared that day.

Now yer take dat an' go. Put that in the book. Yer kin make out wif dat. I ain't a gonna tell yer no more. Nosir. The end a time is at hand anyway. 'Tain't no use ter write a book. The Bible say when it git so's yer cain't tell one season from t'other the worl's comin' to end; here hit is so warm in winter that [HW: it] feels like summer. Goodbye. Keep lookin' good an' come again.

450002

Interview of Miss Mary Jane Wilson
Portsmouth, Virginia
By—Thelma Dunston

NEGRO PIONEER TEACHER OF PORTSMOUTH, VIRGINIA

One of the rooms in the Old Folks Home for Colored in Portsmouth, Virginia is occupied by an ex-slave—one of the first Negro teachers of Portsmouth.

On meeting Miss Mary Jane Wilson, very little questioning was needed to get her to tell of her life. Drawing her chair near a small stove, she said, "my Mother and Father was slaves, and when I was born, that made me a slave. I was the only child. My Mother was owned by one family, and my Father was owned by another family. My mother and father was allowed to live together. One day my father's mastah took my father to Norfolk and put him in a jail to stay until he could sell him. My missus bought my father so he could be with us."

"During this time I was small, and I didn't have so much work to do. I jus helped around the house."

"I was in the yard one day, and I saw so many men come marching down the street, I ran and told my mother what I'd seen. She tried to tell me what it was all about, but I couldn't understand her. Not long after that we was free."

Taking a long breath, the old woman said, "My father went to work in the Norfolk Navy Yard as a teamster. He began right away buying us a home. We was one of the first Negro land owners in Portsmouth after emancipation. My father builded his own house.

72

It's only two blocks from here, and it still stands with few improvements."

With a broad smile Miss Wilson added, "I didn't get any teachings when I was a slave. When I was free, I went to school. The first school I went to was held in a church. Soon they builded a school building that was called, 'Chestnut Street Academy', and I went there. After finishing Chestnut Street Academy, I went to Hampton Institute. In 1874, six years after Hampton Institute was started, I graduated."

At this point Miss Wilson's pride was unconcealed. She continued her conversation, but her voice was much louder and her speech was much faster. She remarked, "My desire was to teach. I opened a school in my home, and I had lots of students. After two years my class grew so fast and large that my father built a school for me in our back yard. I had as many as seventy-five pupils at one time. Many of them became teachers. I had my graduation exercises in the Emanuel A. M. E. Church. Those were my happiest days."

PREPARED FOR PUBLICATION
BY
HISTORIC PUBLISHING
SAN ANTONIO, TEXAS
©2017 All Rights Reserved

Slavery Books & African American History Courses & Resources
https://africanamericanhistorybooks.blogspot.com

WWW.HISTORICPUBLISHING.COM